BROADWAY PLAY PUBLISHING, INC.

SUMMIT CONFERENCE

by

Robert David MacDonald

249 WEST 29 STREET NEW YORK NY 10001 (212) 563-3820

SUMMIT CONFERENCE

First printing: July 1983

ISBN: 0-88145-009-X

Cover art by Bill Sloan, Three.
Design by Marie Donovan.
Set in Baskerville by BakerSmith Type, NYC.
Printed and bound by BookCrafters, Inc., Chelsea MI.

SUMMIT CONFERENCE was first performed on 20 January, 1978, at the Citizens' Theatre, Glasgow, by the Citizens' Company, for whom it was written. The play was directed and designed by Philip Prowse, with the following cast:

A SOLDIER: Gary Cooper
EVA BRAUN: Ann Mitchell
CLARA PETACCI: Julia Blalock

The first London performance was given at the Lyric Theatre, Shaftesbury Avenue, produced by Colin Brough for the Lupton Theatre Company Ltd., on 28 April, 1982. The play was directed and designed by Philip Prowse, with the following cast:

A SOLDIER: Gary Oldman
EVA BRAUN: Glenda Jackson
CLARA PETACCI: Georgina Hale

The American premiere of SUMMIT CONFERENCE took place on March 10, 1981 at the Tufts Arena Theatre, Boston, Mass. It was directed by Laurence Senelick. The cast included:

A SOLDIER: Chris Polsonetti
EVA BRAUN: Daina Robins
CLARA PETACCI: Kayla Black

Boys throw stones at frogs in sport;
but the frogs die in earnest.

Plutarch

ROBERT DAVID MacDONALD was born in Elgin and trained originally as a concert pianist. Since 1973 he has been an associate director of the Citizens' Company, Glasgow, for whom he has written 20 translations and seven plays, as well as directing the British Premieres of Lermontov's *Maskerade*, Balzac's *Vautrin*, and several plays of Goldoni. Among his many translations are: Rolf Hochhuth's *The Representative* and *Soldiers*; Goldoni's *Country Life*; and, most recently, Genet's *The Balcony, The Blacks*, and *The Screens*. His version of *War and Peace*, in the production by his former teacher, Erwin Piscator, ran for two seasons on Broadway and won an Emmy Award when televised.

INTRODUCTION

Indifference makes accomplices of us all, and we are responsible for other people's actions in a precise ratio to our power to prevent them happening. Every generation, therefore, has events with which it must come to terms if it hopes to walk a straight path afterwards. For my own, immediately post-war generation, the destruction of the European Jews—Holocaust seems an over-emotive if convenient shorthand—was just such an event.

In our century, the human imagination, the faculty hitherto considered boundless, has had some severe strains put on it. Man has begun to accept facts as he hears them, much as, formerly, he might have made an Act of Faith about an ecclesiastical dogma. But if a writer fails to confront his material with a fairly steady gaze he will fall into sentimentality, aestheticism or self-indulgence.

A glance at any airport bookstall will show that this is no barrier to success, but it plays havoc with any serious claim to consideration. It is all too easy to appreciate the play of light, color and form in the mushroom cloud hanging over the stricken city because the enormities taking place beneath it are no longer possible to grasp. The concept of race-murder, though hardly an invention of our century, is one which surfeits even the ghoulish appetites of those who wait for every new air disaster to be the worst in history—and how many of us are quite free from that feeling?

The idea that the fate of a people—several peoples indeed—lay at one time in the hands of a bunch of mediocrities who might otherwise, but for the accident of power, have lived out shabby, slightly dotty but relatively harmless lives as shady perverts in some South Coast resort, is one we reject as unimaginable, which makes it all the easier to ignore, to forget.

The mind is first sickened, then numbed, and finally stages a withdrawal from the experience. We can visit Auschwitz today much as we can the Colosseum, and the horrors of each are equally remote from us.

But what is a dramatist to do with material which has made the statuesque horrors of the Jacobean playwrights both more real and more ridiculous, but which, after the lapse of a scant generation, has been politely rejected, to become the stuff of vicarious erotic fantasy? Clearly a newsreel documentary presentation is no longer effective: Hitler might be as remote as Tamburlaine. Recitals of statistics impress with their detachment but quickly grow wearisome in a narrative medium. Expressionist generalisations, alienation effects, and punches below the emotional belt to engage our private emotions at the expense of understanding, are all as ineffective as they are well-intentioned. The necessary fictions of the stage make any realistic presentation of the unthinkable—well, unthinkable. What then?

My own professional involvement with the Third Reich, so to speak, began in 1963, when the veteran director, Erwin Piscator, asked me to Berlin for the final rehearsals of a new author's first play, Rolf Hochhuth's *The Representative*. Working on the Berlin and subsequent London productions of the play left me with the uncomfortable feeling that sooner or later I would have to come up with a Third Reich play of my own. But Hochhuth had exacerbated the situation for anyone who followed him, by writing what, after nearly twenty years, still strikes me as the most important European play since the war it deals with, the play which restored the theatre to its place as a platform for judgment and prophecy.

The reality of our time is no longer to be conveyed in private situations. In an age where a concept has arisen of the individual's role in society which permits him to live out his entire life without feeling the necessity to reflect on the nature of good and evil, let alone make much of a choice between them, there has to be a broadening of the dramatic objective. We have to see the battlefield where the conflict is to be decided, and the forces that will decide the conflict.

This may sound a rather hyperthyroid introduction to a work of such relative slightness as *Summit Conference* but, if mountains are not always delivered of mice they are certainly delivered of smaller hills and *Summit Conference*, where not the product of circumstances, was the product of rejection and selection of the available possibilities. After directing a production of *The Representative* in Austria, after addressing numberless Jewish groups, arguing in halls, on TV, in bars, with Catholics, Jews, neo-Nazis, and just plain cranks, I realized that only some form of *distance* would lend, if hardly enchantment, then at least detachment to the view.

I wrote a play about the Marquis de Sade, under the illusion that it was a diaphanously-veiled allegory on the Nazi state, but the notoriety of the central character deluded people that it was all about sex. (Not the first time the two have been muddled.)

Finally, after watching countless films exploiting the pornography of that particular vileness, I saw a re-run on TV of Lubitsch's *To Be or Not To Be*, and remembered that in ancient Greece a tragedy's theme was repeated in a parodistic or ironic treatment.

The fact that a comedy, of whatever sort, on the subject of the most monstrous event of our lifetimes, an event, moreover, in which I had been spared personal involvement, might be construed as cynical impertinence bordering on blasphemy, could be outweighed by the fact that, for once, the material would not be surrounded by that penumbra of taboo, which induces a critical aphasia, a sort of emotional paralysis, in the audience. The idea of such an appendix to the theme, which might round off my own involvement with the subject, although energetically discouraged by sensitive liberal acquaintances, stuck naggingly in a corner of my mind.

When, in 1976, the director Philip Prowse asked me to write a two-character play for the Citizens' Company of Glasgow, about the mistresses of Hitler and Mussolini having tea (a fiction—they never met: Scott Fitzgerald held that "Biography is the falsest of the arts") while their lovers carved up the continent in the next room, excuses for not writing it seemed to have run out. I nevertheless objected that two-handers never worked without excessive recourse to that most banal of stage properties, the telephone, and that plays with one-sex casts always degenerated into either jockishness or bitchery, and perhaps one male performer would not spell fiscal doom? That agreed, it remained only to write it and hand it over to the team that produced it, in the event, impeccably.

The fact that it has not entirely exorcised the subject for me may indicate that the play has not entirely done the job I wanted it to do. Perhaps there are too many targets; perhaps the stance appears over-ambiguous. At times the politics crowds out the feminism: at others the reverse. But all subjects worth writing about have a tendency to acquire for me a barnacle incrustation of satellite subjects. This may indicate a grasshopper mind, but grasshoppers, while hardly deep thinkers, certainly get around.

The first act has been accused of being a history lesson but, forty years after the play is supposed to take place, there must be enough people for whom, without some factual exegesis, the practical acting-out of the theories in the second half would be incomprehensible. To the better informed, my apologies. To the know-it-alls, my sympathy. For the rest, I hope it may provide a footnote, if no more, to our understanding of that time.

Finally, I have to thank Rolf Hochhuth, one of the few living writers entitled to call himself 'protest-ant' for putting me to all this trouble, to whom I dedicate this satyr-play in friendship and admiration, and who I hope will accept the echo of the central moment in his play which occurs towards the end of mine, with the pinning-on of the Star of David, as a tribute of homage and affection.

R.D.M.
London, April 1982

ACT ONE

A high-walled room in the Chancellery in Berlin. Dotted around are several scale-models of buildings in the style of Albert Speer. The lack of windows conceals the fact that it is summer, 1941. A telephone rings and the SOLDIER *appears. He answers the telephone.*

SOLDIER: Ja . . . jawohl . . . When are they going to begin? *(Pause)* Good fucking question! About time too! *(He goes back to his place and waits. Sound of a sentry marching up and down outside. Enter* EVA *by another door.* THE SOLDIER *gives the Hitlergrüss.* EVA *looks a bit non-plussed and gives a confused salute back.)*

EVA: Cushions?

SOLDIER: Cushions, gnädige Frau?

EVA: Cushions. My cushions. The ones . . . I made them for the F . . . for my fr . . . for the birthday last week.

SOLDIER: I shall inquire, gnä' Frau.

EVA: I am not a married woman, you know.

SOLDIER: No, gnä' Frau.

EVA: Then you do not need to address me as one.

SOLDIER: No, gnä—

EVA: Chefin will do.

SOLDIER: Chefin.

EVA: Chefin, the feminine chief, you understand? You needn't look so scared—in all probability you will never use it again. After today, that is.

SOLDIER: Very good, gnä—Chefin.

EVA: Now just fetch those cushions.

The SOLDIER *exits.* EVA *shows signs of nervousness. She switches on the radio, gets music. Goes to a mirror and makes up her so far colorless face. Hums a number, e.g. 'Ten cents a dance'—in German. Lights a cigarette, looking around before she does so. The* SOLDIER *enters with two cushions, embroidered with swastikas. She hides her cigarette—too late.*

EVA: The true German woman does not smoke, is that it?

(No answer)

How old are you?

SOLDIER: Nineteen . . . Chefin.

EVA: A good age for testing your beliefs. On sound evidence When is my guest due?

SOLDIER: She will be delivered at five o'clock.

EVA: I want to see her arrive. I want to see her car.

She goes to the door.

SOLDIER: *(Blocking her exit)* I'm sorry, Chefin.

EVA: What do you think you're doing?

SOLDIER: I have my orders.

EVA: I swear to thee, Adolf Hitler, as Führer and Chancellor of the German Reich, loyalty and bravery unto death, as God is my judge. Do you like this music?

SOLDIER: Is it American?

EVA: I expect so. Do you like to dance?

SOLDIER: Would I . . . ?

EVA: I said do you, not would you?

SOLDIER: Sometimes, Chefin.

EVA: Nineteen and modest. Ambitious too?

SOLDIER: I only wish . . .

EVA: Oh don't bother. You only wish to serve your Fatherland and its glorious leader to the best of your ability and the last drop of your blood. Have you any brothers or sisters?

SOLDIER: Nine, Chefin.

EVA: Really not? Oh, I understand—*(Bitter)* How lucky for you and your mother. She has, I assume, been awarded the cross of German motherhood?

SOLDIER: First class.

EVA: Of course. I expect you like dogs, too.

SOLDIER: We have a dog at home.

EVA: A German shepherd? Naturally. An ideal family. You will go a long way, if not far. Oh, why are Italians always late for everything? They are as bad as the Austrians, I mean the Viennese. "All right on the night, Professor." Italy was even late for the war. Have you heard this riddle? What is the difference between Julius Caesar and Mussolini?

SOLDIER: I don't know.

EVA: Caesar came, saw, and conquered. Mussolini came when he saw someone else had conquered. I think a sense of humour is terribly important in wartime.

SOLDIER: It's very clever, gn—Chefin.

EVA: They boast that he made the trains run on time. Perhaps it is just the women who are late nowadays.

SOLDIER: A German woman is still a German.

EVA: What else would she be?

SOLDIER: I don't know, Chefin.

EVA: A little thought before you speak then.

(Noise off)

EVA: Is that her now?

The telephone rings. The SOLDIER *answers it.*

SOLDIER: Ja ... jawohl ... am   Apparat ... Ja,   Herr
Obersturmbannführer ... nein ... the Führer and the Duce
have just gone into the conference room ... sehr gut ... the
service elevator? ... nein, Herr Obersturmbannführer ...
not at all funny ... jawohl ... zu Befehl ... auf wiederhören.

EVA: The Duce is a guest in our country. You should mention
him first. Manners are very important. Well?

SOLDIER: Frau Chefin's guest will be here at any minute.

A knock at the door.

EVA: At last. Herein!

The SOLDIER *salutes. Enter* CLARA, *very done-up.*

CLARA: 'Ow terrible to be so late. You must forgive ... *(Notic-
ing the* SOLDIER*)* Oh, in Rome we salute higher. *(She shifts his
arm)* So, cara, how lovely to meet you at last. I missed you
when you were in Naples before the ... all this began. You
made a great impression. La bella bionda.

*(*EVA *salutes)*

Oh, tesoro, I know it is supposed to be unhygienic, but this
once ... *(She kisses* EVA*)* Sorella. I feel we know one another
very well already.

EVA: I'm so glad you could come.

CLARA: And the scenes I had to make to do so. But such a
comfortable train. Until after the frontier.

EVA: I'm sorry. Perhaps you would like some tea. *(To the*
SOLDIER*)* You may serve tea now.

CLARA: *(As the* SOLDIER *exits)* So nice to see something rather than that dreadful brown all the time. What a peculiar colour to select. Why not blue? It don't suit Italian men, but with fair hair and . . .

Eva: It was the national colour of Bavaria. Where I come from.

Clara: Oh. You mean it would have looked provincial? Red? No, of course not. Black? Already taken. What about white?

Eva: We would think it effeminate.

Clara: Really? How quaint. Well, brown it had to be, I suppose.

Eva: Like the earth.

Clara: Of course. Would you like a cigarette?

Eva: German women don't smoke.

Clara: Then whose is the butt in the ashtray? Don't tell me that nice boy has been smoking. At his age? And on duty? And with lipstick? I thought you had got rid of that sort of thing, even in the SS. Come, don't make me smoke alone.

Eva: Well, perhaps. I have to be so careful. My friend doesn't like the smell.

Clara: Really? How amusing.

Eva: Why?

Clara: My friend likes me to smell all the time.

Eva: What of?

Clara: Oh, scent, my body, anything strong. He is very passionate, if not for very long at a time.

Eva: I . . . I must take your photograph.

Clara: Oh, no, please. I must look terrible.

Eva: I can't imagine you looking better.

Clara: Oh, I can, I can.

EVA: Never mind, this is an important occasion, and I don't suppose it will be repeated. I love to take photographs, don't you?

CLARA: I am no good at it. I always cut people's heads off. Maybe you can leave that to your . . . I mean, I prefer to just have the experience.

EVA: But don't you like to be reminded?

CLARA: Not much. And if I do I can go to confession. Except, of course, I always forget half what I mean to say the moment I kneel down. Typical.

EVA: We have our own church in Germany now.

CLARA: We have always had our own church in Rome.

EVA: My friend says the Pope is very difficult to deal with.

CLARA: Pacelli? No, no. He is so worried about the Russians and being made a saint, he gives no trouble to anyone. He is also . . . you know . . . pederast.

EVA: I don't believe it.

CLARA: Of course not. You put them in prison, don't you?

EVA: Yes, we do.

CLARA: I'm surprised you still got an army.

EVA: *(With a camera)* Now hold still.

CLARA: Oh no, really. Well, then at least from my good side.

A flash as the picture is taken.

EVA: There, all over. Now you must take one of me.

CLARA: But I tell you, I am all thumbs at it.

EVA: We have wonderful cameras in Germany. You just press this little button and it does all the work for you.

CLARA: But . . .

EVA: I insist. You must. They're all I have. Without them I
could be living on the other side of the moon. The whole
world knows I am here, and nobody knows who I am. I
sometimes wonder myself, Who I am. Fräulein No-Private-
Life. My friend promises me when the war is over I shall go
to Hollywood to play myself in the film of his life—but they
will probably say I am too tall for the part. Part. What part?
I make a frame to go round something that isn't there. I watch
American films that are forbidden, I listen to American jazz
which is forbidden, to convince myself I am privileged to be
unlike other German women. And to make myself even more
unlike them, I smoke, I drink, I wear make-up, I shave my
armpits. I make lists of my jewels and pretend ignorance of
the bodyguards who are set to watch me—at least they know
I am there—and nightly I receive the greatest man in the
world, and that is very nice, even if he leaves me afterwards
so as to be found in his own bed by his masseur in the morning.
Also I have tried to kill myself; three times so far. The courtiers
court me, and their wives hate me, and laugh at me behind
my back, because I am not even allowed to arrange the meals
at the Berghof. Which are disgusting. My parents ask me, in
concerned and quiet tones—"Why doesn't he marry you?"—
and I tell them they are ridiculously conventional for the
modern age, and that marriage with a dictator can only be
morganatic at the best; but I am conventional too. I match-
make for my sisters, for their dogs even, I whistle 'Tea for
Two' with obvious intent, and my friend tells me I have got
the tune wrong, and I end up saying he is too dedicated, too
ascetic, married to Germania, but it hurts me all the same,
when he says—"After the war there will be a German husband
for every German girl"—and I cannot even have the same as
my sisters, or any other wide-hipped Aryan, Bavarian cow.
Do you know my greatest moment of triumph? As I watched
the special train pull out taking that English lord's daughter,
the one who shot herself for . . . taking her back to England
before they could accuse us of having had her assassinated.
The foreign press even got a picture of that, but there was

no picture of me. Then I came home and took out my 23 albums of photographs. And there I was. And all those important people whom I am never allowed to meet. When the Duchess of Windsor came I had to stand on the lavatory seat to get a shot of them. I wish it had been a gun. But the pictures are there, and the future will know who I am . . . was. So . . . Please?

She gives the camera to CLARA.

CLARA: Ma cara, of course, if you want it so bad. Just press this little button? Where do you want to stand?

(EVA *roams around to find a position*)

For me, I don't really care what happens. I have a nice apartment on the floor above his office, with a deaf attendant, because, you know, my friend shouts quite a lot when he . . . then afterwards he likes to play the violin, he plays very well, not Heifetz, of course, but for a politician . . . is that where you want to stand, cara? Now don't blame me if this is no good. Promise?

(*As she aims the camera the* SOLDIER *enters with a tea trolley, etc.* CLARA *swings round and flashes the camera at him*)

Oh, dear, I told you. I'm sorry. Still . . . (*To the* SOLDIER) . . . it will be a nice picture of you. (*Looking at the laden trolley*) Madonna mia, who else is coming?

SOLDIER: Coming, signora?

CLARA: (*Flattered*) Oho, signora! Yes, all those cakes, who are they for?

EVA: I'm sorry, I thought you would like something to eat.

CLARA: I only dare eat a little bread and butter. My line. I am not so optimistic as you must be.

EVA: (*To the* SOLDIER) Can you take a photograph? Here, just press this. Wait! (*She sits down and starts to pour the tea*)Milk?

CLARA: No, thank you.

EVA: Sugar?

CLARA: No.

EVA: *(Passing a cup to* CLARA) Now! *(A flash as the picture is taken)*

CLARA: *(Spilling tea on her skirt)* Ehi. Diavolo!

EVA: Oh, how dreadful. But it won't stain. *(To* SOLDIER) Run and get a cloth.

The SOLDIER *exits.*

CLARA: *(Mopping with a handkerchief)* No, it doesn't matter. It is not much. Oh, he's gone. Very obedient. Like a little dog. Very nice. I like to have a little dog. Duce laughs at him, but I think he likes him really.

EVA: I miss my two little terriers so much. Stasi and Negus. They are in the country at the moment. It is so difficult to get enough for them to eat. Still, I always say if my friend is a vegetarian then somebody should have his meat ration. But he does not like them. He says they are ridiculous. He never allows me to take a picture of him with them. And they hate that terrible Blondi, his big shepherd dog.

CLARA: Why do they have this passion for big dogs? You ever notice how Churchill and Roosevelt have tiny ones? The American one, Tralala or whatever he is called, it looks like a flea with hair.

EVA: Degenerates and cripples! How can they win a war? The Americans will not come into it, why should they be interested, until it is too late for them. As for the English, they have had their time. They had no ideals left, and this is a war of ideals.

(The SOLDIER *enters)*

Oh, thank you. It is all right now. Beautiful shoes.

CLARA: Ferragamo.

EVA: Oh, so are mine.

CLARA: Duce does not like me to wear high heels. They make me taller than he is. When we are standing up, of course.

EVA: Really? Won't you have some cake?

CLARA: *(To the* SOLDIER, *who hands her a plate of bread and butter)* Oh, look, how thoughtful of him.

EVA: I'm so sorry I didn't think of it myself.

CLARA: But cara, you were being a wonderful hostess.

EVA: I get so little opportunity. Some more tea?

CLARA: Thank you.

EVA: *(To the* SOLDIER) We shall need some more hot water. Oh, there is some. Very well, that will be all. Thank you.

SOLDIER: I shall be outside it you need me, Chefin.

EVA: And if I don't?

(No reply)

Thank you.

The SOLDIER *exits.*

CLARA: He is really very attentive.

EVA: Yes.

CLARA: And attractive.

EVA: I expect so.

CLARA: How old is he?

EVA: I really have no idea.

CLARA: It is wonderful to be surrounded by the young. Wonderful to grow up and see the world becoming younger as you watch.

EVA: To have something to believe in. Something to make sacrifices for.

CLARA: You understand about politics?

EVA: I don't think a woman has to understand things. As long as she knows them.

CLARA: You think we would be sitting here if that were true? You think I do not know what that attentive attractive boy is doing outside this room? He is there to stop us getting out. Am I right? Or did you think he was there to prevent us from being disturbed? At what, for heaven's sake? I had to make as many scenes to get here as you must have had to make to be allowed to ask me here to tea like an English lady. I have to travel in a separate carriage from Duce; I live on a separate floor of the hotel; I am delivered here to the back door like the bread, and I come up in the service elevator. My biggest satisfactions so far, you know what that has been? I lend Duce's daughter Edda—Ciano—a diamond bracelet, which will not suit her at all, for the reception this evening to which you and I will not be asked. You think you are First Lady of Germany? Perdonami, I forget, apart from Germania. And you want to be moral, like Mary Pitchford in the movies. Cara, you are a scandal. Duce is married, to a peasant woman, who has given him six children, na, maybe five. Edda looks a bit Jewish, they say, still . . . now she can't think of anything else to give him except big meals, which, with his stomach, he don't digest so good anymore. But I am Duce's whore, and that is what they call me. I am there all right. I am a scandal, but at least I am a public scandal. Every month I give 200,000 lire to the poor, and they look at my clothes and they smell my scent and they spit—and take the money. My family and my friends are well-placed. People come to me thinking I have influence with Duce. They think I intervene, but I do nothing. Sometimes they get what they want, and are grateful, if not . . . well, what matter. I lie on the divan, looking at the ceiling, or I paint my toenails different colours and cut pictures out of the film magazines and paste them in my scrapbook: Lana Turner, Gina Artur, Myra Loy. And I wait for Duce. They say I am making a rag out of him, that he got no ass in his trousers any more, but they don't dare tell *him* anything. Sometimes we are happy, and sometimes we quarrel, like when I laugh at him for the way he stands clutching his balls all the time, against evil eye, malocchio you know, as if he was afraid they were going to be struck by lightning. Don't laugh, cara, I seen your friend on the newsreels—he stands like that too. What's he doing? Covering up the German unemployment problem? Ha, ha, ha. No, cara, we both wanted men, and we got institutions, spooks born of a million minds. And maybe we shall have to swing for them. Gangsters, cara, that is what they are, all of them, and gangsters are only interested in two kinds of women: mothers and whores, especially Italian gangsters. So here I am. It is like the war. The big countries are whores, and they better start learning to behave like them. If they want to stay alive. And us. Now, you got something to drink?

EVA: More tea?

CLARA: No more tea, thank you.

EVA *pulls open a colossal, astoundingly stocked drinks cupboard that is concealed in the wall.*

EVA: You'd better come and choose.

CLARA: Ehi, ma che selezione! Oh, ma guarda, I haven't had this for years. *(She pulls out some vile-colored French liqueur.)* Not since before the war.

EVA: But then, you didn't conquer France, did you?

CLARA: Cara, that was not a nice thing to say. Chin-chin. Oh, but you're not drinking. You don't smoke, you don't drink. What do you talk about at confession?

EVA: There is no more room for the church in the Reich.

CLARA: I hope your friend isn't silly enough to have that opinion.

EVA: It is his opinion.

CLARA: Then he'd better keep it in the family. He should be grateful to the Holy Father. The signing of the Concordat with the Vatican was the first time his government got any credit abroad. Oh, good. *(As* EVA *reaches for the bottle)* You keep me company.

EVA: We're all the company we've got.

CLARA: There is always that nice boy outside.

EVA: Later, perhaps. Give me a cigarette.

CLARA: But of course. I am corrupting you. You will see, you will become a wicked woman like me. Except, of course, you are one already. *(Clinking glasses)* Deaf and blind lives a hundred years. How long are they going to go on?

EVA: But they only went into the conference room five minutes ago.

CLARA: No, I mean your stupid war.

EVA: What do you mean, ours?

CLARA: Duce never wanted it. Not till next year.

EVA: He took long enough to come into it.

CLARA: He was trying to keep you out of it. Why does your friend not listen to Duce any more?

EVA: The Führer's destiny speaks with a louder voice.

CLARA: Oh, come on, cara. It's me you're talking to. Not a public meeting. Politicians only talk about Destiny when they've just made a mistake. Destiny is like sex . . . people talk about it more than they believe in it. I tell you why you he no longer listens to Duce. Because he never stops talking himself. Last time they met he talked for two and a half hours without stopping. Duce was so exhausted he came home and broke two strings on his violin and tore my bra strap . . . playing *Humoresque.*

EVA: There are moments in history when vertigo seizes every waking, thinking man, and in such moments only the sleepwalker can be sure of his step. We are at such a moment now, and Adolf Hitler guides us with the assurance of a sleepwalker.

CLARA: You are talking like a book.

EVA: I got it from a book. His book.

CLARA: Cara, I got to admit something. It may be called *My Struggle*, but it's a bigger one for the reader. I never finished it. And nor did Duce.

EVA: Perhaps if he had done he would not be so discontented now. Though what he has to complain about, I'll never know. The greatest army the world has ever known has just won the greatest battle in the history of the world, at Kiev. The wireless says 300,000 dead. And where is your friend in all of this? He has sent ten divisions, and crates of apples saying 'Sunshine from Italy'.

CLARA: Ten divisions that could have decided the war in Africa for us.

EVA: Why are you so old-fashioned? To fight a colonial war? It's too late by a hundred years. They took away our colonies in 1918—the British will lose their empire soon.

CLARA: And what is left over the Americans will buy.

EVA: And you'll be at the pierhead at Naples selling it to them. I am sick and tired of hearing about the Americans. They will not enter this war, whatever Mr. Roosevelt tells them. They will be content with lease-lending a few old destroyers they don't know what else to do with. Let them go on making their wonderful films, even if we cannot see them here. Oh, but I have a copy of *Gone With the Wind*. Maybe you will like to see it this evening? If they are still talking.

CLARA: Ooooh, *Via col Vento*, marvellous! Vivian Legg. But Duce will not declare war on America. Too many Italians. It would not be popular.

EVA: The Italians in America are all trying to pass for pilgrim fathers now. Anyway, you will have to declare war if we do. We are allies, or had you forgotten?

CLARA: It is not difficult to forget sometimes, when we are

never informed of what is going on. I am surprised we were told about Russia, even if it was half an hour after the invasion began. And you know what he did, Duce, when he heard the news? He telephoned his wife, from my apartment, never had he done such a thing before, he has to much taste, and he said to her: "Mamma"—you see what he calls her—"Mamma," he said, "the war is lost."

EVA: Then you will have lost it with us, if not for us.

CLARA: Hope you let us know when you decide to surrender.

EVA: Have you ever seen a shadow survive the sun which throws it?

CLARA: How dare you talk like that to me!

EVA: You can make it a pleasure, dear.

CLARA: You know what's wrong with you Germans? You always go too far, but you never know how far to go. One German: a philosopher; two Germans: a public meeting; three Germans: a world war. And then you have nothing left, and have to begin All Over Again.

EVA: Better than one Italian: a tenor; two Italians: an opera; three Italians: an army in retreat. Ha, ha, ha. Don't you think that's funny? Terrible to be without a sense of humor.

CLARA: Even more terrible to live somewhere where you need one so bad.

EVA: You know what they're saying? The English have got a secret weapon—the Italian army. Ha, ha, ha.

CLARA: Well, why didn't he attack England, and not Russia? He has the biggest army in the world, what was he frightened of, getting his feet wet? Doesn't he read the history books? Hasn't he heard of Napoleon?

EVA: Let England wait with her cricket and her Jews. The empire in the East has been our dream for six hundred years.

CLARA: And a war on two fronts has been the nightmare of your generals for the last hundred of them.

EVA: Two fronts. And whose fault is it that we are now fighting on three? Your insane invasion of Greece compelled us to come to your assistance. If anyone is responsible for the losing of this war, it will have been you. There is only one country which can afford to fight a war on three fronts.

CLARA: And that is . . . ?

EVA: Switzerland, In eighteen months, no twelve, our armies had swept Western Europe into the sea, and then what do you do? Well, you declare war, I admit, like a vulture declares war on a dead zebra. Without even mentioning it to me, you open up some idiotic colonialist adventure, and because we have given our word we have to come and save you from being made to look ridiculous.

CLARA: Well, you never mentioned to me you were going to invade Rumania; you never said you were going to invade France. You never even said *when* you were going to invade Poland. I got more information from the newspapers than from your ambassadors. What's the matter? Don't you trust me any more? I thought: "Now let them learn what it feels like."

EVA: How like a woman.

CLARA: When you went into Austria I did nothing although it meant goihg back on my word of five years before. You loved me then. "Never, never, never will I forget this," you said. "I shall be ready to go with you, through thick and thin, no matter what happens, I shall stick to you, even if the whole world were against you."

EVA: I said that?

CLARA: You think I made it up?

EVA: I wouldn't put it past you. I sometimes wish I'd never met you.

CLARA: You'd be looking pretty silly if you hadn't. I was a passport to respectability for you. For eleven years I had led the Italian people; I was the most admired politician in

Europe, the one who got things done. Even the railways, I made . . .

EVA: Yes, you told me, repeatedly.

CLARA: Everyone admired me. Lord Rothermere compared me to Napoleon. Even in 1939 the *Manchester Guardian* called me the greatest statesman of our time. Bankers, cardinals, the Archbishop of Chicago, Fiorello La Guardia, von Papen, Briand, Puccini, all praised me. Winston Churchill said: "If I were an Italian, I should don the black shirt."

EVA: He had every opportunity to put one on in England at the time.

CLARA: Even you wrote to me asking for a signed photograph.

EVA: Why didn't you send me one?

CLARA: I did not think fit to accede to your request.

EVA: Well, if you had it would be hanging in the maid's room by now . . . as a warning. I need a cigarette.

CLARA: Help yourself, as if you wouldn't. You spoil everything. The first time we met, I thought: "Look at that frightful yellow macintosh. He looks like a plumber, standing on the platform with his felt hat in his hand." I thought: "I suppose I should be pleased that someone else has carried out a revolution on our lines, but they are Germans and will end by ruining everything." And so you have. Fascism is not for export. Points of view don't travel well. You are still Huns, Lutherans, enemies of Rome, and you will always be. You take everything and make it worse, and then blame us for having the idea in the first place. Look at that thing. (*Pointing to one of the architectural models*) What's that thing supposed to be?

EVA: The Victory Arch on Unter den Linden.

CLARA: Well, that's one you won't have to build then. Even that you take from us. You never seen the railway station in Milano? Make that look like public lavatory. Why you didn't attack England? Bloody people: they invite Haile Selassie to the coronation but not me; they come all over Italy like a rash, stupid old women feeding the cats, and pansies with titles or titled cousins, seducing the waiters. You ever see Venice in September? Everywhere you look, bored boys whispering: "Amore, amore, amore," like a stuck record of a parrot, and a lot of tweed heaving away. I mean, it's all very well, but it's impossible to get a gondola till mid-October.

EVA: England and Germany are natural allies. I do not know why we had to fight them. Their stupid guarantees to Poland. How were we to know they would not be as worthless as those they gave to Prague? An axis stretching from Glasgow to Naples, no other nation would have dared say 'peep'. Three nations, pledged to the destruction of Bolshevism and its Jew-led hordes. There is one question on which Churchill and I see eye to eye.

CLARA: Not now.

EVA: No? What can he do for Stalin? He will be only too glad to have the pressure taken off him. The English are too phlegmatic and self-righteous to be woken up by anything except brute force. Leave them alone and the only things they will object to are parliamentary indiscipline, a corrupt police force, and malpractice at the Foreign Office.

CLARA: One thing they don't forgive is being frightened. And that's what you have done. I never made that mistake.

EVA: If you frightened anyone it would have to be by mistake. I march into Vienna, Prague, Oslo, even Paris, without breaking so much as a windowpane, and you . . . you bomb seven colors of shit out of a lot of woolly-headed Abyssinians so as to pretend you have an empire, and a lot of woolly-minded internationalists in Geneva impose sanctions on you, so the only person who will still talk to you is me.

CLARA: And mamma mia, how you talked.

EVA: A pity you didn't listen more closely.

CLARA: Not at all. All the others listened to what you said.

I watched what you did. You were a simpleton in politics. You called yourself socialists, and a workers' party, and then you smashed the trade unions. You're right, you are like a sleep-walker, you had no great plans for coming to power, any more than you had great schemes for combating economic crisis.

EVA: I knew I would get there. Von Papen and the rest thought I was their prisoner, a useful tool against the tottering Weimar Republic: their plottings brought me to power. The slump which put me there was over by the time I got there, but no one had noticed, they all thought it was due to me. When a peasant decides to grow his little fingernail long one day, and that same day finds a gold piece in a field, he will put two and two together, that's how gods are born. And then no one could stop me. You think the other powers would have thrown me out? I came to power by the legal road. I was democratically elected, and only another equally democratic election was going to remove me. Germany was a great power once more and had to be fitted into the map of Europe, unless they wanted Soviet Russia to take its place. You and I, friend, were and are the last bastion against the Jew-Tartar barba-rians, the hordes of Genghis Cohen. Did I ask for war? I rearmed but so did everybody else. You think armaments produce war? You might as well say umbrellas produce rain. I gave that nice old man with the umbrella my autograph at Munich. Who precipitated the Austrian crisis? The Austrians. Who was the first to begin the dismemberment of Czechos-lovakia? The British; and they were as anxious to persuade Poland to grant concessions as they were to restrain me. They won the Great War. Well, now let them watch me win the Greater.

CLARA: Whores and gangsters, whores and gangsters and whores. Chin-chin.

EVA: Whose fault that Germany became a whore? The traitors of Versailles.

CLARA: Oh, Versailles, Versailles, Versailles, I'm sick of hear-ing about Versailles. It's like people blaming their lack of character on an unhappy childhood? The results are dreadful.

EVA: You should complain. You were on the winning side.

CLARA: That time.

EVA: Thinking of changing? Germany became a whore, spreading her legs for any party who could give her the price of a square meal. At the time Italy was just an ageing countess, offering refreshments to her domestic staff. As a son of Germany . . .

CLARA: . . . adopted son.

EVA: As a son of Greater Germany, I was determined no one should ever call my mother a whore again. I would make people recognize her. By whatever means. They hooted at me, they whistled at me, then I gave them work and that meant bread. Try whistling with your mouth full. The National Socialist movement was the nation's protest against a state refusing them the right to work, and all at once I was the expression of the German people. Grub first, then morality, as a Communist playwright put it, but even a stopped clock tells the truth twice a day. I gave them a morality they could understand, because it was one they could have thought out for themselves if they hadn't been so busy munching.

CLARA: I leave all that to the church. Give them something to occupy their minds.

EVA: In Italy the church rules morality. In Germany the state rules, morally. The only system that will always win is morality strictly applied, and like any other best-seller, it should be a morality which confirms the largest number of people in the largest number of prejudices which they already hold. Most people prefer the revival of former glories to the sacrifices demanded to make new ones. Bismarck had made Germany great, I made her great again. And since they could not bring themselves to believe that Germans could have brought their country so low, I gave them a present: I gave them the Jews.

CLARA: Ahi, Madonna, here we go again.

EVA: And you would have done well to follow my example.

CLARA: Oh, I tried for a while, but nobody took it seriously. I did everything you told me, but they just said: "What is an Aryan? The arse-end of a proletarian." Ha, ha, ha. Take their trousers down, see if they got a . . . you know . . . snipsnip. Anyway, how do you tell? Do they really smell?

EVA: They can disguise themselves as what they like, and God knows I can't tell them from Italians, but I have made them responsible for every ill for which Germans could not take the blame: for Versailles, for Bolshevism, for American capitalism, and for the war. Every race feels itself to be superior—the childhood prejudices of a community can wall one round like a fortress. But superior to what? To those who do not share those prejudices, the free agents, the gypsies, passing through with their light luggage, spilling their filth, and envied, oh, yes, envied, because they represent the wishes and dreams of every man, who would like to be free of responsibility. The Jews are the best allies I have.

CLARA: Why get rid of them, then?

EVA: They are the scapegoat, on whom all the nation's sins are laid, and is then driven out into the wilderness. Even those people liberal enough to have feelings of guilt are not likely to be endeared to the cause of them. No, Liebchen, without the Jews I should as surely have been turned against as the Italians will turn against you. With them I have the connivance of a nation. I cannot recommend them highly enough, and would advise you to find a persecutable minority, of whatever race or creed, before Christmas at the latest.

CLARA: *(Hopefully)* The Red Cross?

EVA: Someone has to be responsible for the way you're behaving in Africa, and it better not be you, or I may start believing it is.

CLARA: Then what happens when you got no more Jews?

EVA: They will last me the war. After that, what is German will be right. And there are always the Russians to start on now.

CLARA: I'm beginning to wish I hadn't come. Damn, the bottle's empty. What else you got?

EVA: You've had enough.

CLARA: Don't be mean. You can afford it. *(At the cupboard)* Eeny, meeny, miney, mo, catch a . . . By the way, what you going to do with the niggers when you're Queen of America? At least you can tell who is and who isn't. *(She pulls out a bottle)* Ahi, guarda, delicious.

EVA: It is so simple, you make sure everyone thinks they are an economic danger, and if possible a sexual threat, and, as everybody thinks he hasn't enough money and doesn't get enough sex, you can safely leave the rest to them. With the odd bit of encouragement, of course.

CLARA: *(Toasting)* Salute, i negri. Salute, gli ebrei. Salute, cunt. Why you never get married?

EVA: I am married, to Germany.

CLARA: Yes, yes, I mean no, no, why you not married to that . . . girl . . . what is her name?

EVA: Only one woman could ever be considered suitable: Winifred Wagner. It would be a national undertaking.

CLARA: More like a mountaineering expedition. I thought she married Toscanini.

EVA: Toscanini? Toscanini has refused to conduct at Bayreuth any more. I was very upset.

CLARA: You see? I keep telling you, you get it all wrong. For me, Toscanini was Fascist candidate. True. 1919. At least when he raise his right arm you know he's going to conduct. Ha. Ha. So, you marry her. "Achtung, achtung, this is the greater German radio. Today, advance parties reached the summit of Signora Wagner's left nipple. With this glorious advance the whole of her left breast may be said to be in German hands. Stay tuned for further bulletins from FHQ: Pom-pom-pa-pom." Musica. Musica. *(She turns on the television set: March music)* Oh, Dio, boom-boom-boom. You would never think the Austrians had invented the waltz.

(The picture appears on the screen)

Ehi, ma che c'è? Santa Madonna. *(She crosses herself)* A little cinematograph.

EVA: A television set. After the war there will be one in every German home.

CLARA: After the war there won't be any German homes. Ehi, look, paso romano, geese-step. Another present from you. I was a fool to accept it. When did it all change? When you came to see me first, I painted all the house fronts from the border all the way to Rome. I looked at you in the motorcade, with rouge on your cheeks, and dandruff on your collar, and I thought 'a clown'. Two years later I came to you and I saw what you had done, the efficiency, the dedication, the inflexibility, and I thought: "This is not my revolution any more; the sorcerer's apprentice has stolen the book of spells." And I felt like a woman, everybody saying how nice I was and how important, but all the time taking second place. Marshal Göring showed me his electric trains, your generals listened to me in awe, as they had probably been ordered to, and a million people on the Maifeld, in the pouring rain, heard me saying: "When Fascism has a friend it will march with that friend to the last." It was a triumph; but it was a woman's triumph. A woman's nature is to copy, and like a woman, when I returned home, I set out to copy you. The first thing I did was to order the geese-step to be the official march of the Italian army. I called it the firm, inexorable step of the legions for whom every march was a march of conquest. But it looked ridiculous.

EVA: It has to be done well. Then it is ideal, rhythmic, noisy, intimidating, and difficult to perform. What more could a warlord require?

CLARA: Difficult? Macchè! Anyone can do it. Look.

(She tries but her high heels betray her, and she falls on the floor)

Oh, I fell over. I am a fallen woman. Ha ha, ha.

EVA: Get up at once.

CLARA: Leave me alone. You don't like me any more.

EVA: Yes, I do, and I've had to do some pretty damn silly things to prove it.

CLARA: You see, you resent me. I gave you the best years of my life, and now look at me. We both thought we'd be gangsters, and we each got a good gang around us. Bang bang bang. It was all right as long as we stayed in our own street. The polizia knew where to find us, and they left us alone. But being a big gangster means you have to fight a big war, and the bigger you get, the bigger the war gets, and the polizia always win in the end, and then you got to go back to being a whore. And that, caro il mio Führer, is something we should do our best to avoid . . . but we shan't.

EVA: Past history seems so clear, a raucous and brightly lit cavalcade, this cause produces that effect, the mill-wheel turns, never churning the same water twice. But the present? The future? I am like a man walking in the night with a lamp on my back, showing the path to those who follow me, but unable to see the path ahead, only knowing that it is there. What I have done was seldom the result of previous wisdom but forced on me by occasion. The only lesson history teaches us is how to falsify it. Will we really lose this war? How can we? It would be a tragedy.

CLARA: Then if you want to be the hero of it, you'd better not survive it.

EVA: Those who win wars are heroes, those who lose wars are martyrs; those who avoid them are . . . nothing. Nobody loves a neutral. I used to think when this was all over I would retire, to Linz, and cultivate my garden, walk the dogs, give autographs, listen to the radio telling me about your continued effective bombardment of Malta . . .

CLARA: Bitch.

EVA: . . . but truth is easier to suppress than reality. It's a bigger target. You're bound to hit it somewhere. But reality?

A pinpoint, changing every fraction of a second. Pushing us all the time into performing parodies of what we meant to do.

CLARA: Don't try to make excuses. You're being maudlin.

EVA: Make a big enough mistake and sooner or later someone will come up with an excuse for it. Make enough big mistakes and sooner or later you become the center of a religious revival. You tell me, look at Napoleon. Well, you look at him. I stood in front of his tomb in the Invalides, 1500 tons of vomit-colored granite, and wondered how the French could ever have put up such a monument to the man who had so exhausted them that over a century later I could get through their defences with no more trouble than climbing a five-barred gate. Then I thought, relics of glory, that's what people want: to be the children of wealthy parents. Relics. Why, I bet you could get a fair price if you auctioned off his cock. If you could find it, that is. I wonder if it was . . . I mean, how . . . you know . . . big . . .

CLARA: Hard . . .

EVA: Well . . .

CLARA: No, I mean hard to tell.

EVA: Ah . . . *(Pause)* Küss mich, mein Duce. (CLARA *kicks off her shoes)*

CLARA: Baciami, il mio Führer.

(A long kiss. A knock at the door, unheeded and repeated. The SOLDIER *enters. On seeing them he retreats at once)*

(As the door closes, but not springing apart) Who was that?

EVA: What can it matter?

(A knock at the door)

Ach, verdammt nochmal. *(She breaks away from* CLARA *and shouts:)* Herein!

CLARA & EVA: *(Together)* You never know.

As the door opens, the curtain falls.

ACT TWO

Everything exactly as at the end of ACT ONE, *except that the* SOLDIER *is standing in front of the now closing door.*

SOLDIER: Will it be all right for me to clear away, Chefin?

EVA: Yes, go on.

(He starts to clear. They watch him intently, EVA *humming a tune. Aware of their gaze on his back, he stops, and turns)*

You can leave the glasses.

He goes back to clearing away. The women look at one another, smile, nod, and come in on either side of him, and sit down, watching him still. He becomes increasingly nervous. EVA *takes a cigarette. He lights a match, just as* CLARA *also takes a cigarette.*

EVA: My guest first.

SOLDIER: I beg your pardon.

(He lights CLARA's *cigarette and blows out the match)*

I beg your pardon.

(He lights another match for EVA)

EVA: Your hand is not very steady.

SOLDIER: I beg your pardon.

EVA: That's quite all right.

SOLDIER: Hat Frau Chefin sonst einen Wunsch?

EVA *smiles but says nothing and turns away. The* SOLDIER *begins to wheel the tea trolley out.*

EVA: Just a minute. Did anyone ask you to go?

SOLDIER: I beg your pardon. I thought . . .

EVA: Don't keep begging our pardon. We shall begin to think you may have done something wrong. Have you?

SOLDIER: I . . . hope not.

EVA: So do I.

SOLDIER: If there is anything I can do . . .

EVA: That remains to be seen. *(To* CLARA) Nicht wahr, Schatzi?

CLARA: Ssssssi, tesoro. *(To the* SOLDIER) Come here. Oh, you've got blue eyes.

SOLDIER: Yes, signora.

CLARA: Unusual. Very nice.

SOLDIER: Er . . . thank you.

CLARA: He's blushing. Ehi. *(She pats his cheek)* Cherubino.

SOLDIER: Thank you, signora.

CLARA: You know what cherubino means?

SOLDIER: No, signora.

CLARA: What you thank me for then?

SOLDIER: I took it to be a compliment. May I go?

EVA: You may not. What are you doing here?

SOLDIER: Looking after Frau Chefin and her guest.

EVA: Then sit down.

SOLDIER: I don't think it's my place . . .

EVA: You're quite right. It's my place. And I'm asking you to sit in it. There. *(She pushes a stool over to him with her foot)*

SOLDIER: Thank you.

EVA: Cigarette?

SOLDIER: I don't smoke, thank you.

EVA: Why not?

SOLDIER: The Führer has said it is dangerous.

EVA: You can always gargle afterwards. I do.

SOLDIER: Very well. *(He takes a cigarette.* EVA *flicks a match for him)* Oh, thank you.

CLARA: You smoke like a young girl on her first night out. Cara, give him a drink.

SOLDIER: No, I . . .

EVA: I know the Führer is an abstainer but he does not object to other people drinking. What would you like?

SOLDIER: Perhaps a beer then.

EVA: Of course. *(She pours him a tumblerful of venomous-looking liqueur)* Here.

SOLDIER: Thank you.

CLARA: Don't you like it?

SOLDIER: It's very good.

EVA: Do you think I'm drunk.

SOLDIER: Of course not, Frau Chefin.

EVA: Does the question surprise you?

SOLDIER: Yes.

EVA: A great deal?

SOLDIER: Yes, Chefin.

EVA: Hardly a question to be expected of someone in a normal condition?

SOLDIER: I suppose not.

EVA: What's all this 'suppose'? If the question was surprising it cannot have been in accordance with a normal condition, am I right?

SOLDIER: Of course, Frau Chefin.

EVA: Therefore I am not in a normal condition.

SOLDIER: Frau Chefin is clearly amusing herself.

CLARA: At your expense?

SOLDIER: I'm a bit confused.

EVA: Let me clear things up for you. If my question was not normal, and I am therefore in an abnormal condition, then it is possibly because I am drunk.

SOLDIER: That could be one explanation.

EVA: Got any others?

SOLDIER: No, Frau Chefin.

EVA: You know, for a girl of your age you haven't much conversation. *(Nobody reacts to the word 'girl')*

CLARA: We have to ask all the questions. Like drawing teeth.

SOLDIER: Did you have a nice tea?

The women laugh immoderately.

EVA: Did you get any?

SOLDIER: There was food in the canteen.

EVA: I don't suppose that was very good.

SOLDIER: There was enough.

CLARA: Where do you live?

SOLDIER: Not far.

EVA: On your own?

SOLDIER: I share a flat with a girl friend, near the Siemens works.

CLARA: Don't the air raids frighten you?

SOLDIER: Not much yet.

EVA: Stay with us. We'll look after you.

CLARA: Black suits you.

SOLDIER: My friend says you can't go wrong with black.

CLARA: *(Smoothing her own inky outfit)* Nooo.

EVA: I like to meet a girl who looks after herself, you know, has self-respect. A lot of Jewish girls really let themselves go once they're married.

CLARA: But you're not married.

SOLDIER: Not yet.

EVA: You aren't Jewish either. Are you?

SOLDIER: Not yet. I mean, no.

CLARA: Two things I can't stand—Jews and newspapers.

EVA: Why newspapers?

CLARA: Why Jews? Ha, ha, ha. Caught you. *(The* SOLDIER *laughs)*

EVA: Is that supposed to be funny?

SOLDIER: I heard another. Do you know how a clever German Jew talks to a stupid German Jew?

EVA: How?

SOLDIER: By phone. From New York. *(Dead silence)*

CLARA: You have nice eyes. Did anyone ever tell you?

SOLDIER: Yes.

EVA: You sure you aren't hungry?

SOLDIER: No, really, not.

EVA: Go on. Try and eat something. Got to keep your strength for the war effort. We'll have something to eat, and a few drinks, and maybe a dance or two, and then we'll see. Have an eclair. That should set your imagination working. Bite. There.

SOLDIER: It's very kind of you. Is this where you live?

EVA: For the moment.

SOLDIER: On your own?

EVA: With my friend . . . *(Aside)* But don't worry about him, just stick with me, I'll see you're all right.

SOLDIER: It's very unusual, isn't it? The room.

EVA: I like it.

SOLDIER: Oh, yes, I mean, it's very nice, and very . . . well, unusual. *(Indicating the model)* What's that?

EVA: The Victory Arch through which the Führer will lead his armies in the parade the day the war is won.

SOLDIER: My friend says that if the Russians are beaten . . .

EVA: What do you mean 'if' . . . ?

SOLDIER: When, I mean, then no German will ever have to sweep a street or empty a dustbin again.

CLARA: What about the Italians?

SOLDIER: Well, they're different, aren't they? It's very warm in here, isn't it?

EVA: Why don't you take your jacket off? Let me help you. That better?

SOLDIER: Mmm.

(CLARA puts on a record)

That's nice. Is it American?

EVA: I expect so.

SOLDIER: I thought you weren't allowed to have American music now.

EVA: You just need the right connections. Would you like to dance?

SOLDIER: Do I . . . ?

EVA: I said would you, not do you.

SOLDIER: Well, I don't think . . .

EVA: Dance with me, if you want to keep my business.

SOLDIER: I think I've had a little too much to drink.

EVA: Never mind. Just follow me. No, let me lead. What are you thinking of?

SOLDIER: Your friend's very attractive, don't you think so?

EVA: I can't say I've ever noticed.

SOLDIER: Not German though . . .

EVA: And that makes all the difference?

SOLDIER: Well, yes, I suppose . . . I mean, of course. Quite a lady-killer, I expect. Have you known one another for a long time?

EVA: Never mind that now. And you're trying to lead again. Let me do the leading around here.

SOLDIER: Sorry.

CLARA: Time was when to dance with me was the greatest honor you could wish for.

(She turns the music up loud and goes into a lavish solo dance. The SOLDIER *laughs)*

EVA: Stop making an idiot of yourself, and turn that music down.

SOLDIER: I think I want to sit down. I feel a bit dizzy. *(He loosens his tie and collar)*

EVA: All right.

CLARA: Why don't you open your shirt? *(She undoes a few buttons)* Flap it in and out a bit. Doesn't that feel better?

SOLDIER: Cool.

EVA *motions* CLARA *to take off his boots.*

EVA: You're a very nice girl, you know. What are you?

SOLDIER: A very nice girl. *(He giggles)*

CLARA: Do you have anybody special?

SOLDIER: I used to. Not any more though.

CLARA: Quarrel?

SOLDIER: Killed.

CLARA: Poor baby.

EVA: Upset?

SOLDIER: A bit. In an air raid.

CLARA: Still carrying a torch?

SOLDIER: I suppose so.

EVA: You do a lot of supposing, don't you?

SOLDIER: I don't know . . . *(He snivels)* I think I'd like to go
home now.

EVA: Not just yet. You're upset. Have another drink.

EVA *undoes his belt.* CLARA *massages his feet.*

SOLDIER: Die Fahne hoch, die Reihe dicht geschlossen,
SA marschiert mit mutig festem Schritt:
Kameraden, die Rotfront und Reaktion erschossen,
Marschieren im Geist in unseren Reihen mit.
Boom-boom!
(The SOLDIER *laughs.* CLARA *pours another drink into him)*
Zum letzten Mal wird zum Appell geblasen;
Zum Kampfe steh'n wir alle schon bereit;
Bald flattern Hitlerfahnen über allen Strassen.
Die Knechtschaft dauert nur noch kurze Zeit.

EVA: Nice soft skin. I like a girl with nice soft skin . . .

While the SOLDIER *goes on humming the Horst Wessel Lied, the other two join in quietly, as* EVA *starts getting her hand down the top of his trousers. The* SOLDIER *suddenly jumps up.*

SOLDIER: Jesus Christ, what the fuck's going on around here?

CLARA: Foiled again.

EVA: What does it look like?

SOLDIER: I mean, what are you trying to do?

EVA: Don't start going all virginal on me. What do you think you were asked here for, your conversation, your sparkling repartee, your profound thinking? If I want any of that, I can provide it myself, and if I can't I'm certainly not going looking for it with some brainless little tart who'd be lucky to make 50 pfennigs for a knee-trembler under a railway arch on a good night.

SOLDIER: I don't now how this started. I'm not . . .

EVA: I didn't notice you objecting to being given a nice time? *(To* CLARA*)* Did you?

CLARA: Nope.

SOLDIER: What do you think I am?

EVA: We know what you are . . .

CLARA & EVA: *(Together)* We're just arguing about the price. *(Hilarity)*

SOLDIER: But I didn't know that was what you wanted.

EVA: You opened the box, now you're frightened to look inside. Well, you needn't worry. It's empty. The bats all flew out. God, I despise women. Five minutes and you can't call your soul your own.

CLARA: The Mohammedans don't think they've got souls.

EVA: Well, they've a good point. I wish I had a few of them on my side. And why haven't I? Because . . . *(Rounding on* CLARA) . . . your wretched troops, when not actually in flight, spend their ample spare time making Hackfleisch of the North Africans. My God, I've paid dearly for your friendship. Imperialist.

CLARA: Sticks and stones can break . . .

EVA: Don't interrupt. It is intolerable to be dependent on a inferior being for the procreation of warriors. Intolerable that a creature whose mind cannot encompass anything outside of what she wipes, wears, or whelps, should be the necessary companion of the man of will. But there it is. Women are essential in politics. Where they go, the men will follow, and the women will go where the strongest leads. All over Germany, women breathe my name at their first kiss, groan and sigh it at the moment of sexual climax, and shriek it in childbirth. They tear their blouses open as I pass. They tattoo swastikas on their navels. They fling themselves in hecatombs in front of my car in the hope of being injured and consequently consoled by me. They have proposed I revive the droit du seigneur within the feminine units of the Party. My morning mail contains enough erotic suggestions to curdle the loins of an anchorite, and now just what makes you think you're so different? Different. Diff-er-ent. Yesss . . . there is something different. Just what is it? Do you notice anything?

CLARA: What did you have in mind?

EVA: No, look closely, the shape of the skull. The quality of the hair. There's a certain coarseness, if you look. Something shifty about those eyes. Do you think he looks typically German?

CLARA: He could be Italian.

EVA: Don't be irritating. You know perfectly well what I'm driving at.

CLARA: He has blue eyes.

EVA: He probably has a number of freakish attributes. Amico, the evening is not entirely lost. *(Aside to* CLARA) I think we just got ourselves a Yid. A genuine 18 carat noffkeh.

CLARA: Oh, you'll be seeing them under the bed next.

EVA: You may laugh.

CLARA: Anyway the nose is all wrong, isn't it?

EVA: Details. Details. What one can change, another can change back. *(To the* SOLDIER) Why were you sent here today?

SOLDIER: To look after you.

EVA: And how did you imagine you would do that?

SOLDIER: I don't know exactly. I supposed you would tell me what you wanted.

EVA: Suppose. And did we?

SOLDIER: Yes.

EVA: And did you? *(No reply)* No, you did not. Did you swear an oath of obedience at any time?

SOLDIER: Yes.

EVA: Repeat it, would you?

SOLDIER: I swear to thee, Adolf Hitler, as Leader and Chancellor of the German Reich, loyalty and courage. I swear to you, and . . . and . . .

EVA: Yes?

SOLDIER: . . . and those in authority delegated by you . . .

EVA: Obedience till death, etcetera, etcetera. Thank you. Not made a very good start have we? Who are your parents?

SOLDIER: I was brought up in an orphanage.

EVA: You told me you had nine brothers and sisters, and an Alsatian. I really don't know what to believe. Are you ashamed of your parents?

SOLDIER: No.

EVA: Why?

SOLDIER: Why?

EVA: Why are you ashamed of them?

SOLDIER: I just said . . .

EVA: I heard what you said, but I am asking you a question.

(The SOLDIER *tries to put his dress to rights)*

What are you up to, fiddling with yourself down there, you dirty little creature? Leave yourself alone. *(To* CLARA*)* I think we may be trying to hide something. Go and have a look. Is it all there?

CLARA *conducts a ladylike but efficient examination.*

CLARA: Not entirely.

EVA: Snip-snip?

CLARA: Snip-snip.

EVA: I thought there'd be something.

CLARA: He could be a Protestant.

EVA: Protestant kiss-my-arse. He couldn't protest enough to get a fly removed from his soup at a five-star hotel. What are you protesting about?

SOLDIER: I'm not.

EVA: Not a Protestant. I see. You are of course aware the true Aryan does not submit, or cause his offspring to be submitted to an operation which has its roots in a ritual sacrifice of a specifically Semitic nature. I must admit, that in the sandy regions such people inhabit, there may be certain practical advantages, and the brave lads of the Afrika-Korps have all my sympathy, but for yourself . . . surely not. Not only that, but you appear, now I come to think of it, to have been masquerading as a member of a sex to which you have only the cloudiest title. Might it not be that your origins are equally the subject of a similar masquerade, I will not say deception? Come, come, we are not monsters. No one is responsible for what he cannot help. Do you belong to a sports club?

SOLDIER: I beg your pardon?

EVA: Sports club. Club for sport. I do not know the Yiddish word for it.

SOLDIER: I used to.

EVA: Used. To. Were there any Jewish members?

SOLDIER: There used to be.

EVA: Used. To. Be. What happened to them?

SOLDIER: They left. One of them hanged himself.

EVA: Why was that?

SOLDIER: He was asked to resign from the club.

EVA: Weren't there any Jewish sports clubs?

SOLDIER: Yes. The Bar Kochba club.

EVA: Did it have Aryan members?

SOLDIER: Hardly.

EVA: No? You say that as if it was a matter of course.

SOLDIER: I only meant it would hardly be likely that Aryans would join such a club.

EVA: As I said, a matter of course. Do you approve of that?

SOLDIER: Certainly.

EVA: Ah. Then if you approve of Jewish clubs excluding Aryan members, it is clear that you can hardly protest, to use your words, at there being clubs for Aryans without Jewish members.

SOLDIER: I suppose not.

CLARA: Suppose, suppose.

EVA: Then do you not think it somewhat out-of-hand to hang oneself because one is not allowed to belong to a German club? Arrogant. I should call it. What would you call it?

SOLDIER: Arrogant, I supp—arrogant.

EVA: Quite apart from the fact that it is the German, not the Jew, who is on his own soil. If we permit the foundation of Jewish clubs, the Jew must, or should be thankful for such permission. Shouldn't you?

SOLDIER: But I'm not a Jew.

CLARA: I think that is something you should allow your superiors to decide.

EVA: I shall decide who is a Jew or not, as Göring says.

SOLDIER: But you said no one could be responsible for what he cannot help.

EVA: Indeed I did and I say it again. That does not mean we can allow irresponsible elements to run loose in society as they please. Even your Jew-doctor Freud has stated that sexual deviation is a diseased condition rather than a criminal. Does that mean we are to allow such mentally sick people to roam around, infecting the healthy mass of German manhood? No, they belong in hospitals, or rather, since they are not bedridden, in places where they can be looked after without becoming a danger to other people. (To CLARA) How'm I doing?

CLARA: Prima.

EVA: Then you might pay a bit more attention. You could pick up a thing or two.

CLARA: The Holy Father looks after all such questions for me.

EVA: I imagine even you have more political prisoners in your civil jails than in the dungeons of the Inquisition.

CLARA: Well, yes . . .

EVA: Then don't get all holier-than-thou with me. *(To the* SOLDIER) Now then, back to our little problem. Have you ever seen a black woman?

SOLDIER: Yes. In a film.

EVA: Have you ever had a black woman?

SOLDIER: No.

CLARA: Wouldn't you like to?

SOLDIER: I don't know.

EVA: You don't know?

SOLDIER: How can I know if I never tried?

EVA: My dear child, I never tried to play the violin, but I know well enough I can't play it. *(To* CLARA) You will bear me out there. That seems hair-splitting on a Talmudic level. Can you not see such people are different?

SOLDIER: What people?

EVA: Black. Women.

SOLDIER: Different from us. Yes.

EVA: Different from Aryans, I meant.

SOLDIER: Yes.

EVA: Yet even you don't know whether or not you would want to . . . I must say, I am astonished. Surely it is as much against natural law to couple with a different species as it is with the same sex. That was one thing I thought Jewish law was abundantly clear on—the **Book** of Deuteronomy lays down quite strict rules for your guidance.

SOLDIER: I have never read it.

EVA: I can respect someone whose faith is religiously pursued, however erroneously. But laxity is mean-spirited and timid.

SOLDIER: But I'm not a Jew. I am a German.

EVA: A horse that is foaled in a cowshed is still no cow. Don't make it harder for us. Don't force us into measures which even the church has given up. Believe me, I would be happy for the Jews to stay in Germany; one Jew is more use in the munitions industry than two or three foreign prisoners. You speak our language, don't go in for sabotage, and we haven't the trouble and expense, which God knows we can at the moment ill afford, of transporting you all the way from . . . wherever. Don't you see, it is for your protection to live with your own kind? *(She pins a yellow star onto his chest.)* If you were to walk onto the street now, how far do you think you would get? Where would you go to? Whom could you appeal to? How would you get anything to eat? Hold on to a faith, and death is glorious. If it is not a joke. *(She puts her arm around his shoulder.)*

SOLDIER: Death?

EVA: Sit down now. No one is going to die here. You've had a shock. You feel humiliated, frightened, degraded. It's natural that your feelings about what is right should have been a little confused. But you must have faith.

SOLDIER: Faith? In what?

EVA: There is always a choice. But freedom is not the end: it is the means, and a means that must be strictly controlled and dominated if we are ever to establish the ideal kingdom on earth. The world will never get any better without faith. Of course people will suffer, they always have and they always will, but they will suffer to a purpose, and that's the great thing in life, now, isn't it?

SOLDIER: *(A faint struggle in her arms)* I am still German.

EVA: The Jews are more conscious of their race than ever before since the Diaspora. That is our doing. While they lived here, masquerading as Germans, they thought of themselves as Germans. Their German windows were broken in, their German names were eradicated from the bases of German war memorials, they scrubbed German pavements with German toothbrushes on their German hands and German knees.

Now they have nothing left but their Jewishness. I have done more for the Jewish consciousness than anyone since Arthur Balfour.

CLARA: Will they be grateful?

EVA: Ah. Gratitude. Never expect it, particularly from orphans. *(To the* SOLDIER*)* Now sleep. Sleep. I have taken doubt away. No doubt, no hope. No hope, no hate.

CLARA: Cara, you were wonderful.

EVA: Didn't notice you being much help.

CLARA: You seemed to be enjoying yourself.

EVA: Enjoying? Enjoying myself? I feel physically and emotionally drained. You don't know how tiring it is. Not only to get the connivance of the nation, but the compliance of the victim as well. But how else can you punish someone who does not feel guilt? A child must be told something is immoral before he knows. Otherwise punishment would have no effect. They would resist.

CLARA: Don't they?

EVA: Resist? Them? Not much! The force of History is against them. And Morality. The really big lie, even when it has been proved false, will always leave traces of doubt behind, like dust in corners. Once punishment becomes legal it becomes first logical, then accepted, and finally deserved. No man has a really clear conscience when he opens the door to a policeman.

CLARA: Cara, a shithouse is a shithouse . . . *(Pointing to the models)* . . . even if you build it to look like that.

EVA: How typically Italian of you to say so.

CLARA: How typically German of you to point it out. Cara, I have been meaning to say for some time . . . that bow . . . if you were to wear it . . . just a little . . . may I? . . . *(She adjusts an ornament on* EVA*'s dress)* Oh dear, such a difficult material. *(Air raid siren)* Ehi, Madonna mia, what is it?

EVA: An air raid.

CLARA: What are we going to do?

EVA: Stay right where we are. Women of our sort should present a united front.

(The telephone rings. EVA *answers it)*

Ja . . . am Apparat . . . wir werden selbstverständlich der Einladung des Führers Folge leisten . . . Auf wiederhören. *(She hangs up.)* The great men have left the conference room the for bunker. I said we would follow. It has always been my dream that from one of the British planes we shall shoot down, a parachute will blossom, and land in the garden of the Chancellery, and it will be Clark Gable.

CLARA: *(Sighing)* Eeehi.

EVA: The only man who does not need a costume to be a hero.

(Drone of aircraft approaching)

There is no one to stop us leaving now, you know.

CLARA: Then don't you think we should?

EVA: Even Leslie Howard . . . But no, a little . . . too weak, to deserve the love of a woman like Scarlett, a woman able to stand alone against the world, until she meets . . . I like to surrender myself to illusion.

CLARA: When you do that you have only one hope left . . . to create a myth.

EVA: Then let us create one. Men live by myths. But women create them. Men are such perfectionists. But they have no eye for detail.

CLARA: *(Pointing to the* SOLDIER) What about him?

EVA: A myth that will outlast all of us. Villains become victims and victims become villains. In twenty years, who knows? Every age needs both.

(A bomb falls in the distance)

CLARA: Was that a bomb?

EVA: Flak, more likely. Maybe they hit Clark Gable's plane. I think I shall go and put on some lipstick. For Clark.

CLARA: *(Looking at the* SOLDIER) Still . . . pretty.

EVA: Oh, my dear, if you want a meaningful relationship, choose one that will last, something good and destructive—final.

CLARA: Frankly, Scarlett, I don't give a damn.

EVA: Oh, fiddle-de-dee. Tomorrow is another day.

(They retire to the background. A colossal explosion rocks the room. The SOLDIER *wakes.)*

SOLDIER: My name is Hannah Weintraub. I am nineteen years of age. I was born in Wroclaw, known also as Breslau. Before the war, my parents, God rest their souls, ran a small chicken farm, like Reichsführer SS Heinrich Himmler. My native tongue is German; I speak also Yiddish, some Polish, and Hebrew enough to follow the services. I do not know how I came to be here. No. That is not true. I do not want to say how I came to be here. People will ask that in thirty year's time, forty year's time—why did they do it? Why did *they* let it be done? Let them find their own answers. They may need them. "No man," says a Rabbi, "may turn the bones of his father and mother into spoons."—secure in the knowledge that his audience already feels a natural check to such a form of economy. But the check is only felt, it is a sentiment. But . . .

What if the market for spoons were to expand enough for someone to say, "Why not?" and to argue that human progress lay precisely in such an application of material? A law would be needed—no one permits such things unchecked, even without sentiment, and, in an office one day an unimportant clerk picks up a rubber stamp and prints the Aleph, the first letter in the alphabet of destruction whose X, Y, and Z are the ruined watchtowers of Belsen, Maidanek, Treblinka. If I do not mention Auschwitz it is because you will ask for a horror story, which you will begin by not believing, continue by accepting, and end by finding vaguely exciting. Just like anybody else. Such tales may be found in a cheap and convenient form for the pocket in stores where you buy contraceptives and treatises on flagellation, if that is to your taste. Books to be read with one hand, as they say.

There was little in all of it that was new, still less that will grow out-of-date, technique apart, of course. In every country someone within its frontiers is defining a group of fellow-citizens whose actions, while in no way considered criminal at present, are to be in some way restricted; and there, assured by bureaucratic continuity, are the seeds of an efficient killing operation.

The legacy of the Germans is not the atrocity of their program, nor yet the scope even, but the standard they set, which is accepted until it is surpassed. The smoke from the chimneys of the 'bakeries', as we used to call the crematoria in our cowardly way—you would call it 'avoidance'—hides so much of which you can safely say "it isn't as bad as." And anyhow, who remembers? Any more than we remember the 45,000 right hands hacked off the able-bodied men of Gaul by order of Caesar, the 75,000 dead at Borodino, of whom Napoleon said, "One night in Paris will replace them all." Caesar, Napoleon, Hitler—madmen so mad that even madmen say that is who they are. Oh, and the Messiah; of course. Another popular figure.

The West is bright, but with the setting sun: there is no salvation in the East. I will lift up mine eyes into the hills: but from whence cometh help? Good fucking question. Mogen Tuvid, Shield of David, little yellow star, light *my* way; do not shine on Bethlehem.

(During this speech the SOLDIER *has put his uniform back on again, straightened himself up, and now wheels the tea trolley round back to the table, as the women come forward in mid-conversation)*

EVA: I'm so glad you could come.

CLARA: And the scenes I had to make to do so. But such a comfortable train.

EVA: Perhaps you would like some tea. *(To the* SOLDIER*)* You may serve tea now.

CLARA: So nice to see something rather than that dreadful brown all the time. What a peculiar colour to select. Why not white? You seen *The Letter*? Beety Davis? No? We have it already in Roma. Oh, ma che maraviglia. She wears white all the time, and kills this man, her lover or something, but she gets off at the trial, and then they find out it is her, her husband finds out, and she tells him: "Sssssssii, l'ho ammazzato io. E sono felice, ti dico, felice, felice, felice." *(She sighs)* Aahi.

EVA: What does that mean?

CLARA: Eh? Oh, she glad she did it. Glad.

EVA: Glad?

CLARA: Glad. That's right. Then she walks into the garden to certain death. Oh, thank you, a cup of tea. Who do you like best? No sugar. Thank you. Delicious. Tea.

EVA: I used to have a great weakness for John Gilbert. When I was younger.

CLARA: Ah, with Greta Garbo, Queen Christina. You know why she always wear those long dresses? She got enormous feet. Si, ma vero. Ferragamo told me. Biggest feet of all their clients. Your dress—look just like Myra Loy in *When Ladies Meet*. You ever see that one?

EVA: No, I don't believe I did.

CLARA: Ahi, peccato, that Myra Loy, such a beautiful dresser. And so sophisticated. Always a different dress, every time she comes on. Norma Shearer, she wears lovely clothes too. You know she got a terrible squint in real life? Vero. Just sometimes you notice it in the movies too, but only if you know. Of course, she is married to the head of the studio. So I expect it is a bit like us, don't you?

EVA: It must be wonderful to know you're going to be there for ever. Just as you want to be.

CLARA: Ma cara, how can you live if you know the way things will turn out? Duce and your friend, they have made everyone's dreams come true—uniforms and guns and no choices. Well—may I call you Eva?—little girls play with dolls, and grow up and have babies, some of them; but little boys play with guns, and then with themselves, what they going to play with when they grow up? Like I say, Duce and your friend, they have given them everything—like the movies. Right? No cake, thank you.

SOLDIER: The Führer has made history the servant of destiny.

CLARA: *(Nonplussed)* Just what I meant—like the movies. Why don't you try my hat, cara? Give you a chin.

CURTAIN

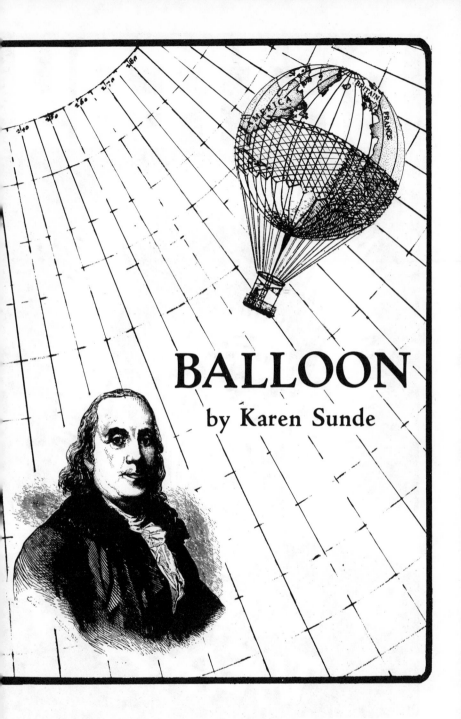

BALLOON

by Karen Sunde

Benjamin Franklin, American Ambassador to Paris during the 18th Century, plays host to his French contemporaries during a festive parlor visit, while the fates of nations hang in the balance.

BATTERY

BY DANIEL THERRIAULT

Electricity is the central metaphor and an expressive image for this unusual love story set in an electrical workshop.

DEATH in the POT

by Manuel Van Loggem

An English-style thriller with a fascinating plot that takes intricate twists and turns, as a husband and wife try to kill each other off, aided by a mysterious Merchant of Death. Mr. Van Loggem's works have been widely produced throughout Europe.

ESCOFFIER
KING OF CHEFS
by
Owen S. Rackleff

In this one-man show set in a Monte Carlo villa at the end of the last century, the grand master of the kitchen, Escoffier, ponders a glorious return from retirement. In doing so, he relates ancedotes about the famous and shares his mouth-watering recipes with the audience.

LOOKING-GLASS

by Michael Sutton and Cynthia Mandelberg

This provocative chronicle, interspersed with fantasy se-
quences from ALICE IN WONDERLAND, traces the career
of Charles Dodgson (better known as Lewis Carroll) from his
first work on the immortal classic, to his downfall when accused
of immortality.

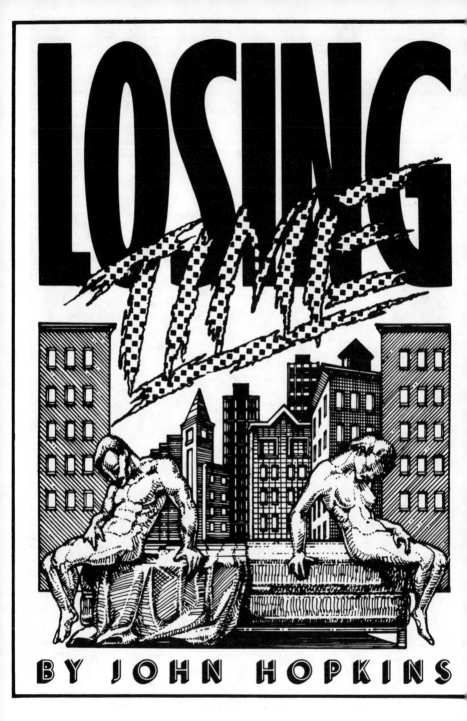

Jane Alexander, Shirley Knight and Tony Roberts won critical acclaim at the award-winning Manhattan Theatre Club for their work in this powerful drama about relationships traumatized by a violent sexual assault. NOTE: Play Contains Explicit Language.

SOME RAIN

by James Edward Luczak

Set in rural Alabama in 1968, the play is the bittersweet tale of a middle-aged waitress whose ability to love and be loved is re-kindled by her chance encounter with a young drifter. First presented in 1982 at the Eugene O'Neill Playwright's Conference and Off-Broadway on Theatre Row.

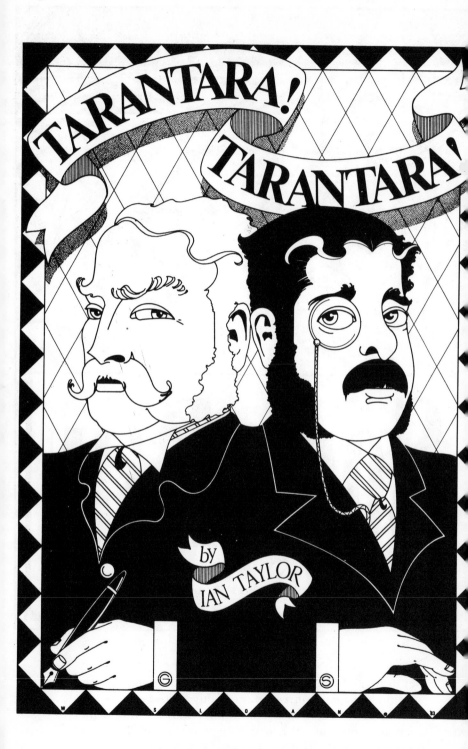